Today Is a Snowy Day

by Martha E. H. Rustad

Pebble®

CAPSTONE PRESS
a capstone imprint

Pebble Books are published by Capstone Press,
1710 Roe Crest Drive, North Mankato, Minnesota 56003
www.mycapstone.com

Library of Congress Cataloging-in-Publication Data
Cataloging-in-Publication data is on file with the Library of Congress.
ISBN 978-1-5157-4919-6 (library binding)
ISBN 978-1-4966-0942-7 (paperback)
ISBN 978-1-4966-0949-6 (eBook PDF)

Note to Parents and Teachers

The What Is the Weather Today? series supports national
curriculum standards for science related to weather. This book
describes and illustrates a snowy day. The images support early
readers in understanding the text. The repetition of words and
phrases helps early readers learn new words. This book also
introduces early readers to subject-specific vocabulary words,
which are defined in the Glossary section. Early readers may need
assistance to read some words and to use the Table of Contents,
Glossary, Read More, Internet Sites, and Index sections of the book.

Printed and bound in the USA.
010060S17

Table of Contents

How's the Weather?

Today is a snowy day.

Snowflakes float down gently.

We look at the forecast.

It tells us how much snow will fall.

How a Snowflake Forms

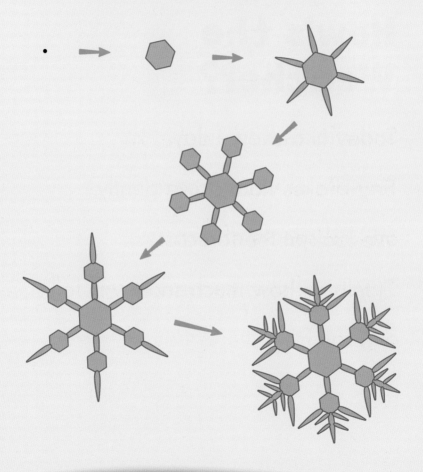

Snowflakes form in clouds.

Tiny bits of water freeze

around specks of dirt.

The snowflakes become heavy

and fall from the clouds.

Each snowflake looks different.

They freeze in different patterns.

Some flakes are bigger,

and some are smaller.

What Do We See?

We see snow all around.

Snowflakes land on buildings,

trees, and the ground.

The snow piles up.

A blanket of white covers everything.

We see footprints in the snow.

Animals leave tracks in the snow.

Cars also leave tracks.

We watch a snowplow clear the road.

A snowy day sometimes turns into a blizzard. Strong, fast winds blow snow around. It can be hard to see anything outside. It is very cold. We stay safe inside.

What Do We Do?

We play outside on a snowy day.
We wear coats, snow pants,
hats, and mittens. We cover
our skin to keep it warm
and dry. Let's sled downhill.

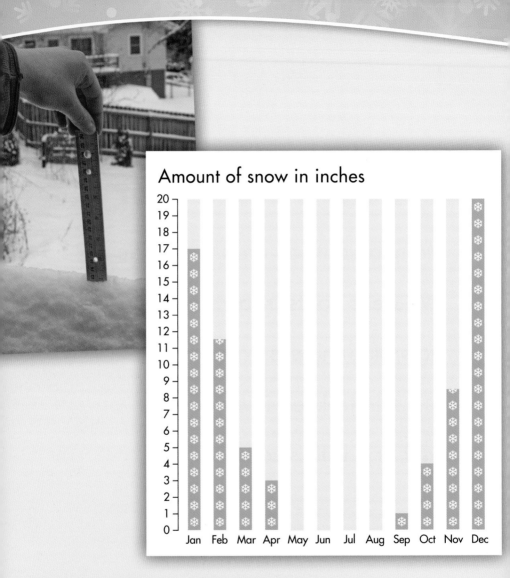

Amount of snow in inches

Month	Inches
Jan	17
Feb	11.5
Mar	5
Apr	3
May	0
Jun	0
Jul	0
Aug	0
Sep	1
Oct	4
Nov	8.5
Dec	20

We measure how much snow fell.
We use a measuring stick. We write
down the amount on a chart.
We see a pattern. Winter has
a lot of snowy days.

We shovel the sidewalk.

Then we go inside to warm up.

We drink hot cocoa.

Look at the snowman we built!

Let's check the forecast for tomorrow.

Glossary

blizzard—a storm with fast winds and blowing snow

forecast—a prediction of what the weather will be

freeze—to go from a liquid to a solid; water freezes at 32 degrees Fahrenheit (0 degrees Celsius)

pattern—several things that are repeated in the same way several times

shovel—a tool used for lifting and clearing snow or dirt

Read More

Bix, Jasper. *Let's Go Sledding!* Winter Fun. New York: Gareth Stevens Publishing, 2016.

Hansen, Grace. *Snow.* Weather. Minneapolis: Abdo Kids, 2016.

Meister, Cari. *Blizzards.* Disaster Zone. Minneapolis: Pogo Books, 2016.

Internet Sites

FactHound offers a safe, fun way to find Internet sites related to this book. All of the sites on FactHound have been researched by our staff.

Here's all you do:

Visit *www.facthound.com*

Type in this code: 9781515749196

Check out projects, games and lots more at
www.capstonekids.com

Index

Editorial Credits
Marissa Kirkman, editor; Charmaine Whitman and Peggie Carley, designers; Tracey Engel, media researcher; Katy LaVigne, production specialist

Image Credits
Capstone: 6; iStockphoto: AwakenedEye, 18 (top left); Shutterstock: BlueSkyImage, cover, JNaether, 12, jordache, 1, 16, Kathy Ritter, 14, Kichigin, 8, kristinasavkov, 18 (design element), Kseniia Neverkovska, cover and interior design element, Max Topchii, 10, MNStudio, 4, Sergey Novikov, 20, -strizh-, cover and interior design element